How People Lived

How People Lived in
Ancient
Rome

Jane Bingham

PowerKiDS
press.

New York

Published in 2009 by The Rosen Publishing Group Inc.
29 East 21st Street, New York, NY 10010

First Edition

Library of Congress Cataloging-in-Publication Data

Bingham, Jane.
  How people lived in ancient Rome / Jane Bingham. — 1st ed.
     p. cm. — (How people lived)
  Includes index.
  ISBN 978-1-4042-4432-0 (library binding)
  ISBN 978-1-4358-2622-9 (paperback)
  ISBN 978-1-4358-2636-6 (6-pack)
 1. Rome—Social life and customs—Juvenile literature. 2. Rome—Social conditions—Juvenile literature. I. Title.
  DG78.B563 2009
  937—dc22

                              2007040221

Cover (main image): A young Roman couple, the woman with a stylus and a holder for writing tablets, and the man with a scroll.

Picture acknowledgments: Map by Peter Bull; Alinari/Topfoto: 10; Keith Collie/AKG-Images: 24; Dagli Orti/Archaeoogical Museum Sofia/The Art Archive: (front cover, bottom) 13; Dagli Orti/Archaeological Museum Zara/The Art Archive: 23; Dagli Orti/Bibliothèque des Arts Décoratifs Paris/The Art Archive: 25; Dagli Orti/Museo della Civilta Romana Rome/The Art Archive: (front cover, middle) 15t, 18t; Dagli Orti/Piazza Armerina, Sicily/The Art Archive: 3, 14; Erich Lessing/AKG-Images: 27t; Erich Lessing/Kunsthistorisches Museum, Vienna/AKG-Images: 9t Erich Lessing/Musée des Antiquitiés, St Germain-en-Laye/AKG-Images: 18b; Erich Lessing/Musée du Louvre Paris/AKG-Images: 11, 26; Erich Lessing/Museo Nazionale Archeologico, Naples/ AKG-Images: 8, 22; NImatallah/Museo Nazionale Archeologico Naples/AKG- Images: (front cover main), 17; Nimatallah/Vatican Museums/Akg-Images: 7; Rheinisches Landesmuseum Trier/AKG-Images: (front cover, top) 16; Rabatti-Domingie/Galleria degli Uffizi Florence/AKG-Images: 27b; Ann Ronan Picture Library/HIP/Topfoto: 4, 5, 9b, 20, 21; Spectrum Colour Library/HIP/Topfoto: 12; Yorkshire Museum, York/Woodmansterne/Topfoto: 19.

Manufactured in China

Contents

Words that appear in **bold**
can be found in the glossary
on page 28.

WHO WERE THE ROMANS?

The first Roman people were hunters and farmers, who belonged to a wandering tribe called the Latins. Around 750 B.C., the Latins began to settle in central Italy. They built villages along the banks of the River Tiber, and over the next few hundred years, these villages grew into a powerful city. The city was called Rome, and its people became known as the Romans.

WINNING LAND

The Romans were excellent soldiers, and they managed to defeat all the surrounding tribes. By 300 B.C., they controlled all of Italy. Then they started to conquer all the other lands around the Mediterranean Sea, including present-day Greece, North Africa, and Spain. In 27 B.C., a powerful leader named Augustus took control of all the Roman lands. This was the start of the Roman Empire.

Extent of Roman Empire

BRITAIN
London
ATLANTIC OCEAN
GERMANY
EUROPE
FRANCE
River Danube
SPAIN
ITALY
Rome
Black Sea
Caspian Sea
ASIA
River Tigris
River Euphrates
Mediterranean Sea
EGYPT
ARABIA
AFRICA
River Nile
Red Sea

◄ A map of the Roman Empire at its largest. The Romans controlled all the lands around the Mediterranean Sea, and also conquered territory in northern Europe.

ANCIENT ROME TIMELINE

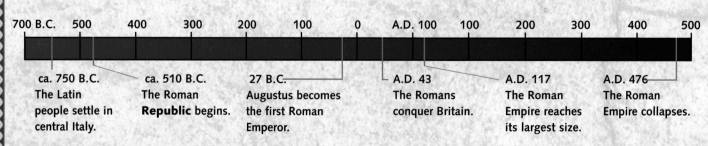

700 B.C. 500 400 300 200 100 0 A.D. 100 100 200 300 400 500

ca. 750 B.C.
The Latin people settle in central Italy.

ca. 510 B.C.
The Roman **Republic** begins.

27 B.C.
Augustus becomes the first Roman Emperor.

A.D. 43
The Romans conquer Britain.

A.D. 117
The Roman Empire reaches its largest size.

A.D. 476
The Roman Empire collapses.

THE ROMAN EMPIRE

The Roman Empire grew rapidly, and by A.D. 117, it had reached its largest size. At this time, it stretched 2,500 miles from east to west, and was home to more than 50 million people. The Empire lasted for 500 years, but by the year A.D. 400, tribes of **barbarians** had begun to attack its borders. In A.D. 476, an army of Visigoths from northern Europe seized Rome and the Empire collapsed.

▼ Augustus the conqueror. In this impressive statue, the emperor wears his army general's uniform.

REAL LIVES

AUGUSTUS: THE FIRST ROMAN EMPEROR

Roman historians describe Augustus as a brilliant army general and a tough, but inspiring, leader. In 27 B.C., at the age of 36, he became the supreme ruler of the Roman world. Augustus gave orders for many grand buildings to be constructed in Rome, but he also passed laws to help the poor. After his death, the Roman people honored Augustus as a god.

ROMAN MEN, WOMEN, AND CHILDREN

Roman society was divided into four main groups: the wealthy upper class, the ordinary working people, the slaves, and the **freedmen** (these were slaves who had become free). Within these groups, Roman men had much more freedom than women.

ROMAN MEN

Roman men were in charge at home. According to the law, Roman men had total power over their wives and children. A man had the right to divorce his wife if she was childless, or if she argued too much. He could even sentence her to death if she tried to leave him for another man. Fathers also had the right to punish their children however they wished.

▲ Wealthy Roman women had their own personal slaves. In this painting, some rich young women are attended by a slave girl.

ROMAN WOMEN

Women did not appear to have power, but they could control how the household was run. Many wives took charge of the family business whenever their husbands went away, and politicians' wives often helped to make their husbands' careers a success.

Upper-class women usually stayed at home and looked after the family, supervising a large staff of slaves. Women from the lower classes looked after their families, and often worked outside the home as well, helping their husbands in their work or taking jobs of their own (see pages 18–19).

ROMAN CHILDREN

The life of a Roman child depended very much on class. Wealthy children had fun at home playing with their toys, and had the chance to go to school. Children from the lower classes helped their parents at work. The children of slaves had to work hardest of all. Most slave children were hard at work long before they were ten. They were given a variety of tasks, from cleaning boots, to serving food at mealtimes.

▲ Most Roman children grew up in large families, and had fun playing with their brothers, sisters, and cousins. This carving comes from a second-century tomb for a child.

REAL LIVES

LATRO: A SLAVE BOY

An inscription on a tombstone in Italy records that Latro the slave died from a snake bite when he was 12 years old. The inscription states that the tombstone was put up by Latro's brother and his fellow slaves. This evidence shows that Roman slaves sometimes belonged to a caring community of other slaves.

WHO WAS IN CHARGE IN ANCIENT ROME?

In the course of their long history, the Romans had two different kinds of rulers. From around 510 B.C., the Roman people belonged to a **Republic**, which was run by a group of **politicians**. However, in 27 B.C., Augustus seized power and the Republic came to an end. After that, all-powerful emperors ruled the Roman Empire.

SENATORS AND CONSULS

During the time of the Republic, the Romans were ruled by the **senate**. This was a group of around 300 men from the most important families in Rome. Senators held regular meetings to make laws for the Roman people.

The Roman senate was led by two **consuls**, who each ruled for two years. The Romans believed that this system would stop any single person from becoming too powerful. However, the Republic broke down when the politician, Julius Caesar, tried to ignore the senate and rule on his own (see panel on page 11). After Caesar's death in 44 B.C., there was a period of **civil war**. Then Augustus took control and became the first emperor.

▶ Senators were rich and powerful men. This statue of a senator holding a scroll illustrates his power to make laws for the Roman people.

ROMAN EMPERORS

During the time of the Empire, Roman emperors were supposed to rule with the help of the senate, but the emperor had all the power, and eventually the job of consul was abolished. Some emperors, such as Marcus Aurelius, were fair rulers who did their best to keep the Empire running smoothly, but others used their power very selfishly. The Emperor Nero spent a fortune on building a golden palace for himself, and gave orders for people who opposed his wishes to be killed.

◄ Emperor Hadrian was emperor from A.D. 117 to 1138, and was an excellent soldier and ruler. He made many visits to the provinces, and built fortresses and walls to strengthen the Empire's borders. The most famous of these defenses is Hadrian's Wall in northern England.

GOVERNING THE PROVINCES

The vast Roman Empire was divided into many provinces and each of these provinces had a governor. The governor's job was to make sure that his province was run smoothly and that everyone obeyed the Roman laws.

REAL LIVES

JULIUS CAESAR

Julius Caesar was a skillful politician and a great army general. He was very popular with the Roman people, and he gradually took control of the Roman senate. In 44 B.C., Caesar declared himself **dictator** for life. This move alarmed many senators and a group of them stabbed him to death.

What was life like in a Roman family?

Most Roman children lived in a large family group, with their parents and grandparents, and their cousins, uncles, and aunts. Wealthy families lived in large, comfortable houses, with many rooms and shady yards. Poorer families lived in very small houses in the country, or in crowded apartment buildings in town.

▼ Rich Roman families often had a town house and a villa in the country. Roman villas were usually built around a garden and were great places for families to relax.

Mothers and fathers

At the head of a Roman household was the father, the *pater familias*. It was his duty to look after everyone in the family home, and to lead them in daily prayers to the household gods (see page 27). However, Roman fathers were often away from home—busy at work or serving in the army—so their wives had to take charge of the family.

Roman women had the task of keeping the house running smoothly. For wealthy women, this involved supervising the household slaves, but poorer women had to run their homes on their own. Mothers made sure that their children were respectful, truthful, and obedient. They also taught their daughters how to be good wives. During the time of the Republic, Roman women of all classes wove all their family's clothes themselves.

ROMAN BABIES

Roman babies were given their names in a special ceremony when they were eight days old. All the family gathered to welcome the child, and wealthy children were presented with a lucky golden charm, called a *bulla*, to protect them from evil spirits.

▶ This family group was carved on a Roman tomb. It shows a mother and father and their baby. The smaller figures are probably household slaves.

REAL LIVES

AN EXCELLENT WIFE

A Roman grave survives from around 5 B.C., with a very long inscription. The inscription was written by a loving husband, who praised his dead wife for her "loyalty, obedience, pleasantness, reasonableness, skill in weaving … and modesty of appearance." The inscription also describes his wife's courage when she stood up to some violent men.

ROMAN CHILDREN

Young children at home had fun playing with their toys. Children from rich families played on seesaws and swings, and a few even rode in miniature chariots. Poor children played with simpler toys, such as balls and spinning tops. Girls had dolls made from cloth, wood, or clay, and boys had wooden swords.

HOUSEHOLD SLAVES

Wealthy families had many slaves to help them at home. Some of these slaves became trusted members of the household, and their children played with the children of the family.

Household slaves looked after the house and yard, and some prepared and cooked the meals. A few educated slaves worked

▲ In this mosaic, a circus boy rides a chariot pulled by peacocks. The toy chariots used by Roman children were usually drawn by goats, and were much safer to ride than this!

as librarians and looked after their master's books, or helped to teach the younger children to read. The master and mistress each had their own personal slaves, who helped them to dress and looked after their clothes.

SLAVES AND FREEDMEN

Slaves were entirely owned by their masters or mistresses, and some of them had terrible lives and worked very long hours. However, many owners were kind to their slaves—they gave them good food and made sure they were cared for when they were sick or old.

Slavery didn't always last a lifetime. Some masters granted freedom to their slaves as a reward for years of loyal service. Freed slaves—both men and women—were known as "freedmen." They had the right to buy their own house and even to keep slaves of their own. However, many freedmen chose to stay with the same family, and continued working for their old master in return for a wage.

◀ A young household slave boy serving food at a banquet, pictured in a mosaic dating from the second century A.D.

REAL LIVES

ZOSIMUS: A HOUSEHOLD SERVANT

The Roman writer, Pliny, had a favorite servant named Zosimus. He was a freedman who entertained his master by reciting poetry and playing the **lyre**. In a letter to a friend, Pliny describes Zosimus as "a good, honest fellow, attentive in his services, and well-read; but his chief talent ... is that of a comedian, in which he highly excels." When Zosimus got sick, Pliny sent him on a country holiday, so that Zosimus could eat good food and recover.

DID ROMAN CHILDREN GO TO SCHOOL?

Children from poor families were expected to work for their living, but richer parents sent their children to school. Roman children started school when they were around seven years old. Girls and boys were taught together in a primary school, known as a *ludus*, and stayed there until they were 11 years old. After that, the girls stayed at home and prepared for marriage, but some boys went to a secondary school, called a *grammaticus*.

EARLY EDUCATION

▲ This Roman carving shows two boys with their teacher. The figure on the right is probably a *pedagogus*—the servant who took the boys to school.

Most primary schools had around 12 pupils, but there were usually many more boys than girls. A servant, called a *pedagogus*, took the children to school and stayed to make sure that they were working hard. School began at dawn and lasted without a break until noon. Roman teachers were very strict, and pupils were often beaten for making mistakes.

Pupils in the *ludus* learned to read and write and do simple sums. They wrote on wax tablets, using a metal pen called a **stylus**. The younger children recited the alphabet and learned proverbs by heart. Older pupils read the works of Greek and Roman authors.

SECONDARY SCHOOL

Boys in the *grammaticus* (or secondary school) studied Greek and Roman literature, mathematics, history, geography, music, and **astronomy**. They also practiced the art of public speaking and trained in athletics.

▶ This young Roman couple are obviously proud of their writing skills. The husband holds a scroll, and the wife holds a stylus and a holder for writing tablets.

REAL LIVES

QUINTUS SULPICIUS MAXIMUS: A BOY POET

Quintus was only 11 years old when he died, but he was already a famous poet. He had won a major poetry competition, in which he beat 52 adult poets. Quintus is known from an inscription on his grave, put up by his proud parents. This evidence shows that some Roman children were very well educated in the art of writing and public speaking.

WHAT JOBS DID ROMAN PEOPLE DO?

The kind of work the Romans did depended on their class and where they lived. Men in the ruling class had the top jobs in government and in the army, and the really hard work was done by slaves. In the countryside, ordinary Romans usually worked on the land, but most people in towns were shopkeepers or craft workers.

SHOPS AND CRAFTS

In towns, many people worked as bakers, butchers, and fishmongers. Carpenters, potters, and metalworkers produced a range of everyday goods, and some skilled workers specialized in luxury crafts, creating fine jewelry, goblets, and ornaments. Roman shops and workshops were usually run as a family business, and children learned their trade by working with their parents.

▶ This Roman carving shows a husband and wife standing by the family knife stall.

◄ Farming in Roman times was very hard work. Here, one man plows a field with the help of two oxen, while the other appears to be gathering fruit.

ROMAN FARMS

Roman farms were usually run by families. Farmers grew crops, fruit, and vegetables, and reared pigs, sheep, goats, and cattle. They also kept flocks of chickens, ducks, and geese. In the warmer parts of the Roman Empire, farmers grew grapes and olives, which they crushed to make wine and oil.

Most Roman farms produced just enough food to feed the family. However, some rich landowners ran huge farms. Food from these farms was sold in markets and even exported to other parts of the Empire.

PHARMACISTS AND DOCTORS

Some Roman men and women worked as pharmacists, and ground up herbs and **minerals** to make homemade pills, ointments, and medicines. Roman doctors gave advice about diet and exercise, and often tried to help patients by draining cupfuls of the patient's blood. Some doctors practiced surgery, and removed **tumors** and even performed delicate eye operations.

ROMAN SOLDIERS

The Roman army provided a good career for adventurous young men. Soldiers were paid well, but they had to spend long periods away from home, conquering new lands or defending the borders of the Empire.

▼ This carved scene of Roman cavalry soldiers comes from Trajan's Column, a monument in Rome. The column is covered with scenes of Emperor Trajan's battle victories.

Most soldiers were **legionaries** who fought on foot, but the Roman army also had some **cavalry** soldiers who fought on horseback. In battle, legionaries fought with long javelins and short swords, and carried large shields to protect themselves. When a Roman army attacked a city, soldiers used a variety of impressive equipment, including huge catapults and battering rams.

Roman soldiers were not just fighting men. They also guarded forts and built bridges and roads to allow the army to move around quickly. Legionaries always traveled on foot. They were expected to march for up to 19 miles (30 kilometers) a day, carrying all their equipment on their back.

CHARIOTEERS AND GLADIATORS

Some young Romans had very dangerous jobs. They entertained the public by racing in horse-drawn chariots, or fighting as **gladiators** in the **amphitheater**. **Charioteers** drove in lightweight chariots, and urged their team of horses to hurtle around a racetrack as fast as they could. Many charioteers died in horrible accidents, but the winners were treated as heroes.

Gladiators fought against each other in bloody battles that often ended in death. Most gladiators were slaves who were taught to fight in special training schools. If they managed to survive for three years, they were granted their freedom. Usually, the chariot drivers and gladiators were men, but there are records of child charioteers and female gladiators.

▲ Two gladiators prepare for battle with almost no armor to protect them. The figure behind them is probably their trainer.

REAL LIVES

FLORUS: A CHILD CHARIOTEER

Florus is known from a grave inscription, where he is described as "a child driver of a two-horse chariot." The inscription says that the gravestone was put up by Florus' loving **foster father**. Florus possibly started life as a slave, but was later adopted by his foster father because of his talent as a chariot driver.

WHAT DID ROMAN ADULTS AND CHILDREN WEAR?

People in the Roman Empire wore very simple clothes, but wealthy Romans loved to dress up and look good. Some Roman women spent hours on their appearance and tried to keep up with all the latest fashions.

▲ In this scene from a Roman painting that dates from the first century A.D., the man and boy both wear togas over simple tunics.

CLOTHES FOR ALL THE FAMILY

All Roman men wore tunics and cloaks, and important Romans sometimes wore a **toga**—a large sheet of cloth carefully wrapped around their body. Togas looked impressive but they were very uncomfortable, so they were kept for special occasions.

The basic garment for women was a long, sleeveless dress called a *stola*. Over this, women wore a *palla*—a large, rectangular shawl—which was sometimes draped over the head like a hood. Fashionable ladies wore bright-colored shawls, made from Indian cotton or Chinese silk.

Roman children wore smaller versions of their parents' clothes. Boys from leading families sometimes wore a toga with a narrow purple border. Girls usually dressed in white until they were married.

HAIR, MAKEUP, AND JEWELRY

In early Roman times, women wore their hair in a simple bun, but by the time of the Empire, fashionable women had their hair curled and braided and arranged in elaborate styles. Most wealthy women used cosmetics. They whitened their faces and arms with powdered chalk, darkened their eyebrows with soot, and colored their lips with plant dye.

Wealthy women wore golden necklaces, bracelets, and earrings, and both men and women had lots of rings. Even poor Romans wore rings made from bronze.

▲ Wealthy Roman women pierced their ears to wear delicate earrings. Gold and pearl drops were especially popular.

▶ Rich women and girls often wore necklaces made from gold and pearls. Poorer women had strings of beads made from colored glass or pottery.

All the jewelry shown on this page comes from a Roman grave in Zara (present-day Turkey). It obviously belonged to a very wealthy Roman lady, because it is made from solid gold.

▲ Many Romans wore signet rings, engraved with a special carving. The ring was pressed into a blob of soft wax, as a way of signing a document.

HOW DID PEOPLE HAVE FUN IN ANCIENT ROME?

When they were relaxing at home, the Romans liked to play games. Children played with marbles and dice, and had a version of tic-tac-toe. Board games were popular, and some of these games had very complicated rules. The Romans also played a variety of ball games. Often, the games involved several players, who used the palm of their hand to hit a small ball.

PUBLIC BATHS

Romans who lived in towns had plenty of entertainments to keep them occupied. All Roman towns had a set of baths, where people went to get clean and meet their friends. Bathers moved through a series of different rooms, each with a pool of a different temperature. In the public baths, people could also enjoy a relaxing massage, a session in the steam room, a workout in the exercise yard, and a swim in the outdoor pool.

▲ A shallow pool from the Roman baths in Bath, England. (All the buildings above the pillars were added later.)

In most public baths, men and women were kept strictly apart. Women went to the baths in the morning, and the men's sessions were in the afternoons. Children were not usually allowed in the baths.

GAMES, RACES, AND PLAYS

The Roman emperors paid for spectacular **games** to be held in vast stone stadiums known as amphitheaters. These violent shows included animal hunts and gladiator fights, as well as brutal public **executions**, when prisoners were mauled to death by lions. Some boys went to the games with their teachers, but girls were not allowed to attend.

As well as going to the games, the Romans also enjoyed outings to the chariot races and the theater. Theater-goers could choose to watch a tragedy, a comedy, or a **mime**. All the actors were male, and they wore masks to show what characters they represented.

▲ This picture shows entertainments inside an arena. It is a copy of a painting found in the Roman town of Pompeii.

REAL LIVES

COMMODUS: EMPEROR AND GLADIATOR

Commodus ruled the Empire from 180 to 192 A.D., but his main passion was the games. Roman writers describe how he sometimes joined in the games, leaving the emperor's box to enter the arena. Commodus liked to give the final death blow to an injured gladiator.

HOW IMPORTANT WAS RELIGION FOR THE ROMANS?

Everyone in the Empire was expected to join in the public worship of the Roman gods. Roman families also held daily services at home. They prayed to their household spirits, and asked them to protect everyone in their family.

HONORING THE GODS

The Romans had dozens of gods and goddesses, but the most important ones were Jupiter and Juno. Jupiter was the ruler of the gods, and Juno was the goddess of women. Soldiers prayed to Mars, the god of war, and children asked Minerva, the goddess of wisdom, to help them with their schoolwork.

▲ In this carving of a religious procession, animals are led to the altar of Mars, where they will be sacrificed to the god.

All over the Empire, there were temples dedicated to the Roman gods. Several times a year, people gathered in front of these temples to watch priests **sacrifice** animals to the gods. Roman adults and children all took part in religious festivals. Some of these festivals were solemn occasions, but others were very lively. At the midwinter feast of **Saturnalia**, everyone exchanged gifts and masters waited on their slaves!

FAMILY WORSHIP

Each family home had its own **shrine**. This contained small figures of the household gods, known as the *lares*. The family gathered for prayers at the shrine, and offered gifts of food and wine to the lares. On special occasions, such as weddings, they gave the spirits extra gifts.

PRIESTS AND PRIESTESSES

In the Roman Empire, being a priest was not a full-time job. Important officials performed sacrifices and the emperor

▲ A shrine to the household gods in a family house in the Roman city of Pompeii. The hollow niche in the wall would have held statues of the lares.

himself was the chief priest. However, one group of priestesses, the **Vestal Virgins**, devoted most of their lives to the goddess Vesta. The Vestal Virgins were chosen by the emperor because of their beauty and good behavior. They began work when they were about 10 years old, and had to live in the temple of Vesta for the next 30 years. Vesta was the goddess of the hearth. The Vestal Virgins' job was to worship the goddess Vesta and keep the fire in her temple burning constantly.

Glossary

amphitheater A very large building where public entertainments are held.

astronomy The study of stars and planets.

barbarians Warriors who tried to invade the Roman Empire.

cavalry Soldiers who fight on horseback.

charioteer Someone who drives a chariot.

civil war Fighting between different groups of people in the same country.

consul One of the two leaders of the Roman senate.

dictator Someone who has complete control of a country.

execution The act of putting someone to death as a punishment for a crime.

foster father A man who looks after a child who is not his own, and acts as a father for that child.

freedman A man or woman who began their life as a slave but later became free.

games Entertainments provided for the Roman people. The Roman games included gladiator fights and animal hunts.

gladiator A trained fighter, who fought battles to entertain the Roman public.

lares The guardian spirits of a Roman home.

legionary A Roman soldier who fought on foot.

lyre A U-shaped stringed instrument.

mime A play performed using silent actions and no words.

mineral A substance found under the earth. Iron, diamonds, and salt are examples of minerals.

politician Someone who plays a part in governing a country.

Republic A period in Roman history when the Romans were governed by the senate.

sacrifice To kill an animal and offer it as a gift to a god.

Saturnalia A midwinter feast during which the Roman people exchanged gifts, and masters and slaves swapped roles, with masters waiting on their slaves.

senate The group of powerful men who governed the Romans during the time of the Republic. The senate met regularly to agree on laws for their people.

shrine A small religious building or an altar where statues of the gods are kept.

stola A loose, sleeveless dress worn by Roman women.

stylus A pointed stick used for writing on a wax tablet.

toga A formal robe worn by some Roman men and boys. Togas were made from a long piece of cloth that was carefully draped around the body.

tumor A swelling or lump that grows in the body.

Vestal Virgin A girl or young woman who served the goddess Vesta in her temple in Rome.

Further Information

Books to Read

If I Were a Kid in Ancient Rome
(Cricket Books, 2007)

Jane Bingham
Ancient Rome
(Wayland, 2006)

Fiona Chandler, Sam Taplin
and Jane Bingham
**The Usborne Encyclopedia of
the Roman World**
(EDC Publishing, 2002)

Peter Hepplewhite
**The History Detective
Investigates: Roman Britain**
(Wayland, 2006)

Philip Steele
**100 Things You Should Know
About Roman Britain**
(Miles Kelly, 2006)

Brian Williams
Ancient Roman Homes
(Heinemann, 2002)

Alex Woolf
**History Journeys: A Roman
Journey**
(Wayland, 2004)

Web Sites

Due to the changing nature of Internet links, PowerKids Press has developed an online list of Web Sites related to the subject of this book. This site is regularly updated. Please use this link to access this list:
www.powerkidslinks.com/hpl/rome

INDEX

Numbers in **bold** indicate pictures.